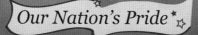

The Bald Eagle

By Karen Latchana Kenney
Illustrated by Judith A. Hunt

Content Consultant:
Richard Jensen, PhD
Author, Scholar, and Historian

magic wagon

visit us at www.abdopublishing.com

Published by Magic Wagon, a division of the ABDO Group, 8000 West 78th Street, Edina, Minnesota, 55439. Copyright © 2011 by Abdo Consulting Group, Inc. International copyrights reserved in all countries. All rights reserved. No part of this book may be reproduced in any form without written permission from the publisher.

Looking Glass Library™ is a trademark and logo of Magic Wagon.

Printed in the United States of America, North Mankato, Minnesota.
092010
012011

THIS BOOK CONTAINS AT LEAST 10% RECYCLED MATERIALS.

Text by Karen Latchana Kenney
Illustrations by Judith A. Hunt
Edited by Melissa Johnson
Interior layout and design by Becky Daum
Cover design by Becky Daum

Library of Congress Cataloging-in-Publication Data
Kenney, Karen Latchana.
 The bald eagle / by Karen Latchana Kenney ; illustrated by Judith A. Hunt.
   p. cm. — (Our nation's pride)
 Includes index.
 ISBN 978-1-61641-149-7
 1. United States—Seal—Juvenile literature. 2. Bald eagle—United States—Juvenile literature. 3. Emblems, National—United States—Juvenile literature. 4. Animals—Symbolic aspects—Juvenile literature. I. Hunt, Judith A., 1955- ill. II. Title.
  CD5610.K46 2011
  929.9—dc22
                    2010013994

Table of Contents

A Strong Bird

Sitting high in a tree is a large, majestic bird.

It stretches out its huge wings. It flies down,

skimming the surface of a river. With its sharp

talons, the bird grabs a fish from the rushing water.

This powerful hunter is a bald eagle. It is a

symbol of the United States. It stands for strength

and freedom.

Bald Eagles in the Wild

Bald eagles are found only in North America. They live by rivers, lakes, and oceans. Bald eagles are raptors. They like to eat fish, reptiles, and small animals and birds.

Bald eagles have very good eyesight. From a tall tree, an eagle can see a fish under the water. Bald eagles build their nests high up in trees. Their nests are some of the biggest bird nests in the world.

A Bald Bird?

How did the bald eagle get its name? After all,

it is not missing feathers on its head.

Bald is short for "piebald." This old word means

to have white markings on a dark body. Hundreds

of years ago, colonists from Europe noticed

the eagle's white head and tail. They called it a

baldheaded eagle.

Becoming a Symbol

In 1776, the United States was a new country. It had just broken free from England. The United States needed a seal. A seal is a picture that is put on letters, important papers, and flags. It stands for a country.

On July 4, 1776, the government asked a group of leaders to make the seal. Three important men were in this group. They were John Adams, Benjamin Franklin, and Thomas Jefferson.

It took many years to work on the seal. Two

more groups tried to get it right. They wanted the

seal to show an animal that lived in North America.

The animal would be a symbol of the United States.

Some people wanted the bald eagle to be the

symbol. Benjamin Franklin disagreed. He thought

the bald eagle acted poorly, as it sometimes steals

fish from other birds. Franklin thought the turkey

was a better bird.

On June 20, 1782, the designers finally finished the seal. It was named the Great Seal. It shows the powerful bald eagle. In an early painting of the Great Seal, the eagle had a dark head. Today, the eagle has a white head.

The eagle is holding objects in its talons and its beak. Each object has a special meaning for the United States.

Symbols of the Great Seal

The bird has a shield with 13 red and white stripes on its chest. They stand for the original 13 colonies that became the United States.

The bald eagle holds arrows in one talon. The arrows stand for power. An olive branch is in the other talon. It stands for peace. A banner flies from the eagle's beak. The banner says *e pluribus unum*, which means "one thing out of many." The United States is one country made of many states.

THE PRESIDENT OF THE UNITED S

Using the Great Seal

When the president signs important papers, a staff member marks them with the Great Seal. The seal also secures the envelopes the papers are put into. The staff member pours wax on the envelope flap. A tool presses the shape of the seal into the hot wax. This keeps the envelope closed.

The president has a seal, too. It is similar to the Great Seal. You can see this seal on the podium when the president makes a speech.

Coins and Dollars

The bald eagle was first put on a coin in 1776. It was a copper penny from Massachusetts. Since then, the bald eagle has been on many coins.

For 115 years, the bald eagle was on the quarter. In 1998, quarters changed. They showed pictures of different states. In 2010, quarters changed again. They showed national parks. The dollar bill also shows the Great Seal with the bald eagle.

Bald Eagles in Trouble

When Europeans came to America, many bald eagles soared in the skies. Since then, the number of these birds has dropped.

Some eagles died from a chemical called DDT. The chemical was in the water they drank and in the fish they ate. It made their eggs weak. The baby eagles could not live. Farmers and fishers also hunted some bald eagles. They thought the eagles stole their livestock and ate too many fish.

Protecting Bald Eagles

In 1940, an important law was created to protect bald eagles. The law made it a crime to hurt the birds or touch their nests or eggs. The chemical that hurt bald eagles was banned. This kept more bald eagles from disappearing from the planet.

24

Bald Eagles Today

Each year, more and more bald eagles are

alive in North America. Some live with other wild

animals in special parks called refuges. Bald eagles

hunt and make their nests there. Park visitors can

see these beautiful birds in the wild.

What the Bald Eagle Means

The bald eagle lives only in North America. Its majestic flight and power have inspired Americans for generations. This truly American bird is a fitting symbol for freedom and for the United States.

Fun Facts

- Bald eagles live longer than most other birds. They can live 28 years in the wild.

- The Great Seal is used 2,000 to 3,000 times each year on important papers.

- A bald eagle's nest can be really big! The biggest one found weighed 2 tons (1.8 t). That is as much as a large truck weighs. It was 9.5 feet (2.9 m) wide and 20 feet (6 m) high. That is only a little shorter than a two-story house.

- Bald eagles fly fast to catch their food. When diving, they can reach speeds up to 200 miles per hour (322 km/h). That's about three times faster than a car on the highway!

- Bald eagles see four to seven times better than people can see.

Glossary

design—to make or draw plans for a certain goal.

majestic—elegant or graceful.

podium—the stand on which a person giving a speech puts his or her notes.

protect—to keep something or someone safe.

raptor—a bird that hunts for meat.

refuge—a park where animals are protected from harm.

skim—to pass over something quickly and lightly.

symbol—something that stands for something else.

talons—sharp claws on a bird.

On the Web

To learn more about the bald eagle, visit ABDO Group online at **www.abdopublishing.com**. Web sites about the bald eagle are featured on our Book Links page. These links are routinely monitored and updated to provide the most current information available.

Index